We Play

We play in the morning.

We play with the soccer ball.

We play with the dog.

We play with the cat.

We play in the water.

We play at the birthday party.

We play with the doll.

We play with the baby.

We play with our mother and father.

We play together.

Note to Caregivers and Educators

Sight words are a foundation for reading. It's important for young readers to have sight words memorized at a glance without breaking them down into individual letter sounds. Sight words are often phonetically irregular and can't be sounded out, so readers need to memorize them. Knowing sight words allows readers to focus on more difficult words in the text. The intent of this book is to repeat specific sight words as many times as possible throughout the story. Through repetition of the words, emerging readers will recognize, and ideally memorize, each sight word. Memorizing sight words can help improve readers' literacy skills.

play

we

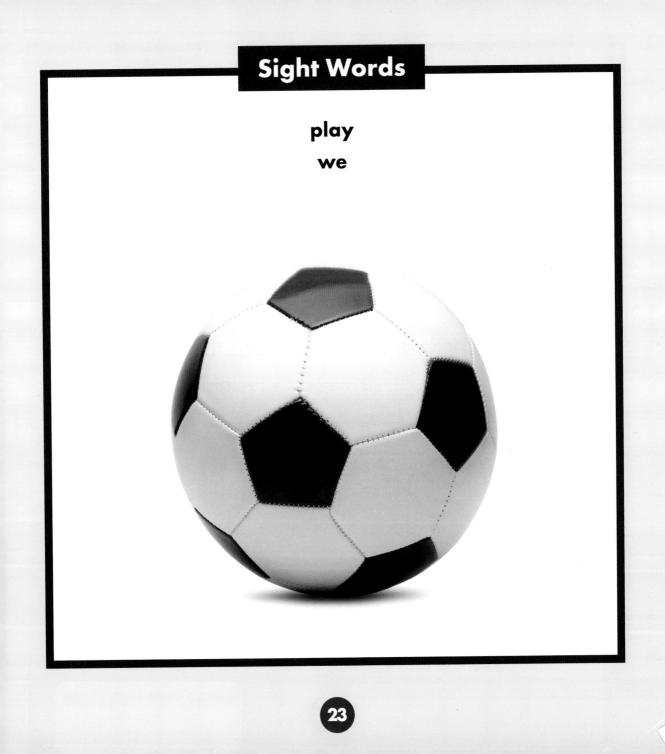

About the Author

Alyssa Krekelberg is a children's
book editor and author. She
lives in Minnesota and enjoys
exploring the great outdoors with
her hyper husky.

Published by The Child's World®
1980 Lookout Drive • Mankato, MN 56003-1705
800-599-READ • www.childsworld.com

Photographs ©: Africa Studio/Shutterstock Images, cover, 1, 5;
iStockphoto, 2, 9, 10, 21, 23; Martin Valigursky/Shutterstock Images, 6;
Robert Kneschke/Shutterstock Images, 13; GPoint Studio/iStockphoto,
14; Ruslan Dashinsky/iStockphoto, 17; Monkey Business Images/
Shutterstock Images, 18

ISBN 9781503835702
LCCN 2019943128

Printed in the United States of America